Real Estate Investing for Beginners

real estate investing for beginners

Start Investing in Real Estate With Little Money and Discover the Secrets to Create Passive Income

Leonardo Williams

Table of Contents

Introduction 5
Chapter 1: Ten Questions a Beginner Asks, Answered 8
    What is Real Estate Investing? 8
    What is the Best Strategy for Me? 9
    How Much Does it Cost Up Front? 9
    Can I Invest Properties I Already Own? 9
    Do I need a Real Estate Agent? 10
    How Do I Choose How Much to Rent for? 10
    Should I Bother with Rentals out of My Area? 11
    How Long Will it Take to Profit? 11
    How Can I Maximize My Profit Margins? 12
    Should I Hire a Property Manager? 12
Chapter 2: Ten Secrets to Avoid Making a Mistake in the Real Estate Market 14
    Don't Waste Money Trying to Learn—Use Free Resources 14
    Don't Skip the Basics 15
    Don't Let Fear Rule You 15
    Don't Choose the First Property 16
    Don't Get Stuck in the Idea of Waiting for a Better Deal 16
    Don't Think that Real Estate Investment is for the Wealthy 17
    Don't Fall in Love 18
    Don't Skip the Planning 18
    Don't Purchase from Unmotivated Sellers 19
    Don't Expect Immediate Results 19
Chapter 3: Investing in Real Estate as a Beginner 21
    What Types of Real Estate Investments Are There? 21
    How Do I Start Making Money? 23
    Active Investing 25
    Passive Investing 27
    Risk Tolerance 28
    Investing without Money 28
Chapter 4: Why Should I Invest? 29
    Cash Flow 29
    Tax Deductions and Breaks 29
    Appreciation 30

Building Equity and Wealth 30
Diversifying your Portfolio 30
Real Estate Leverage 31
Competitive Returns 32
Inflation Hedge 32
REITs 32

Chapter 5: Making Money with the Least Amount of Risk 34

Long-Term Rental Properties 35
Short-Term Rental Properties 36
Buy and Hold Real Estate 36
Real Estate Investment Trusts 37
Diversification 38
Lowering Risks 39

Chapter 6: Evaluating Properties 42

Features of a Profitable Rental Property 43
Features of a Profitable Commercial Property 44

Chapter 7: Tips and Tricks to Selling Properties with Ease 48

Cleaning and Decluttering 49
Invest in Minor Repairs 50
Staging and Boosting Curb Appeal 51
Picking Your Strategy and Sticking to It 52
Knowing the Price and Pricing Accordingly 53
Professional Photography 54
Create a Listing Description 55
Timing the Sale Just Right 55
Be Flexible with Showings 56

Chapter 8: Real Estate Crowdfunding 58

What is Real Estate Crowdfunding and How Does it Work? 59
Benefits of Crowdfunding 60
Disadvantages of Crowdfunding 61
Investment Limits 61
REITs vs. Crowdfunding 62
Is Crowdfunding Worth it? 63

Chapter 9: Common Failures Beginners Face 65

Following Emotions Instead of Numbers 66
Failing to Dedicate Time 67

Quitting Prematurely 68
Not Focusing 69
Skipping Education 71
Skipping the Business Aspect and Skills 71
The Bottom Line 73
Conclusion 74

Introduction

Do you want to make money but don't know how? Are you ready to develop some passive sources of income without having to get so caught up in what you are doing or how you are doing it? If so, you are in the right place… Investing in real estate is a fantastic way for you to start building wealth with ease and all you have to do is make sure that you do so by ensuring that you understand how much to invest and what to do with that investment to ensure that you actually do get to successfully grow your wealth.

Investing in real estate, or in anything, is always a great choice for you—provided that you are using safe investments to ensure that you are actually growing that wealth instead of allowing it to fester or to depreciate. Think about it—even if you put your funds into a savings account, you have a minuscule return. The average savings account will see a return of 0.05% APY. However, inflation goes up significantly more than that each year, with a rate of 3.22%. This means that money that you have sitting in savings is actually *losing* value over time instead of doing anything for you. Instead of allowing it to continue losing value, however, you can start to make it grow instead through investments.

This book is going to focus primarily on utilizing real estate investments as options for you to build wealth over time. This works in a multitude of ways—you are able to build up passive income through the fact that you will be able to take out rental payments. However, you will also be able to earn in other ways as well. You will be able to earn money through building equity on your property, something that happens primarily thanks to the rental payments paying for your mortgage, while you also are able to get the added benefits of appreciation over time as well. Your property will grow in value over time, and as it does, your equity grows as well. In some of the hottest markets in the country, rental values have gone up significantly, and yet there is still a shortage of rental units out there.

When you chose to utilize rental investments, you can generally see yourself gaining a decent return. Your return on investment can even be over 15% sometimes when you look at the values of your property versus what you make, and that means that you can make some significant money if you go through this process, especially if you also make it a point to figure out how you are going to manage your rental.

Of course, you might think that being a landlord sounds too taxing for you—and if that is the case, you are in luck: You can actually avoid having to do so simply by making sure that you utilize a rental management company, which will help you to avoid having to spend more time than you have to. When you contract out to a rental management company, you can protect yourself from constantly dealing with renting out your unit, and all that you will have to do is make sure that you pay your monthly fees.

As you read through this book, you will be guided through understanding the basics of real estate investing, which will grant you the ability to ensure that you *can* make money on the real estate market. You *will* be able to turn a profit without much of a struggle if you know what you are doing, and this book will give you all of the considerations that you will need to make. We will first start out with a list of ten questions that every beginner to real estate investing will ask so that you can begin to get a good idea of what the process is and how it can work out. We will also go over ten secrets to avoid making mistakes on the real estate market as well to make sure that you also protect yourself and your wealth from bad investments. We will take the time to go over the process of investing in the real estate market as well as why you should in the first place. We will discuss the methods that you can use to help you avoid as much risk as possible, as well as how to evaluate and choose out properties that will make for good investments in the first place. We will discuss several different tricks to selling properties to ensure that you can turn a profit, as well as discuss other options, such as real estate crowdfunding. Finally, we will look at the biggest problems that people run into that then lead to them having to make up lost money along the way.

This is meant to be a comprehensive beginner's guide that will help you to ensure that you know what you are doing. This is just the tip of everything—teaching you what to expect so you can then begin to consider making your own investments. If you want to make money on your own, you will need to figure out what it will take and how to invest wisely so you do see the fullest return possible. All of this is entirely contingent upon your ability to become highly successful—it is contingent upon your ability to figure out how you can invest intelligently and how you can make sure that your wealth goes where it should.

There are plenty of books on this subject on the market, thanks again for choosing this one! Every effort was made to ensure it is full of as much useful information as possible; please enjoy!

Chapter 1: Ten Questions a Beginner Asks, Answered

Before we start diving into the ins and outs of real estate investing, you probably want to stop and consider the fact that you do not know very much about it. If you did, after all, you wouldn't be here, looking at a book for beginners. However, there is no shame in that—we all start somewhere, and no one is born simply knowing how to invest or how to make money without learning. We all learn along the way, and the best way to learn is through sheer experience. Of course, to get that experience, you need to dip your feet somehow. This could be through watching someone else invest their money into a property, or you might start small. No matter what, however, you will probably have the same starting questions that we all do.

Within this chapter, we are going to stop and answer the most common questions out there for beginners. If you are done floundering, and you are ready to start making money, then you must start to familiarize yourself with everything that you will need. Through being capable of successfully navigating through these situations, you will start to see that you can actually succeed. Now, let's get started!

What is Real Estate Investing?

Before we begin, let's consider what real estate investing is. Real estate investing is any sort of investment strategy that makes good use of real property—that is, property or land that people live in. It has several different tenets, from purchasing, owning, managing, renting, or selling real estate to make a profit. Some people want to rent out their units to a tenant. Others want to spend time setting up short-term rentals such as Airbnb. Others still want to flip properties, buying them, touching them up, and selling them for a profit. No matter how you chose to invest in real estate, however, one thing holds true: You will be investing your money somehow into property.

What is the Best Strategy for Me?

A common question that new investors ask is what the best investment strategy for them is. They want to know how best to work through the real estate market to make money quickly and who can blame them? We all want to see results as quickly as possible, but that is not always something that is feasible or realistic. The truth is, there are no one-size-fits-all answers here. The right rental strategy for you is largely dependent upon where you live, how much money you have to invest, and how much time you want to spend. It is all dependent upon these variables that matter immensely, and yet no one really wants to deal with them. If you want to be able to figure out the right strategy for yourself, you must first identify the goals that you have and then figure out which method is going to work the best to get you to those goals in the first place.

How Much Does it Cost Up Front?

Now, some people may worry that they need to be rich to invest in real estate. The truth is, however, you can begin investing even with little down on a property. The price will absolutely vary from person to person and will depend upon just how much you are willing or able to spend. It could be very little—you could get a mortgage with little money down. You could also choose to use REITs or crowdfunding to only use a smaller amount of money than you would need to conventionally purchase a house. No matter how much or how little money you have, there is a good chance that you can find something that will help you with your investments.

Can I Invest Properties I Already Own?

Some people wonder if they can utilize properties that they already have, and the answer is actually a resounding YES! If you already have property that you own, then this is actually far easier than if you had to secure it for yourself. When you already have property for yourself to utilize, you do not have to spend the time or effort searching for proper investment, choosing out a property, or trying to secure financing for that property if you are not paying cash for the entire house. This is a perfect option that you can utilize if you do not want to get tangled up with extra financial obligations and already have a house, or if you happen to inherit a house after a parent or family member passes away. This option will actually help you immensely in cutting costs and turning a profit quicker.

Do I need a Real Estate Agent?

Now, while you may not *require* a real estate agent, it is always highly recommended that you utilize them whenever possible. You want to ensure that your paperwork and everything else is just right. Purchasing a property is quite complex thanks to all of the legalities that go into it, and because of that, you must consider what it will take for you to fill out everything on your own. If you do not know what you are doing for any reason at all, then you may want to strongly consider having an agent take care of everything for you. If not, you might still want to do this anyway—having an agent makes things much simpler.

How Do I Choose How Much to Rent for?

Once you have a property to yourself, you may be wondering how much you should charge for rent. This is a tricky question and is one that is largely subjective—the amount that you ought to be paying is typically quite dependent upon just what your property is valued at, market rental rates, and more. Before you begin to advertise your property, you want to make sure that you know what the going rental rate is. You might think that it is actually higher than it actually is and because of that, you can run into major problems. If you are not careful with how you choose to change things around you, you can see huge problems. You must ensure that your fair estimate of the rental value is given. If you charge too much, you are not likely to rent out any time soon. Likewise, not charging enough can cause you to lose out on money that otherwise would have been on the table for you to claim. If you do not want to lose out on that money, you want to charge appropriately and ensure that you are asking for the right amount of money. If you do this the right way, you should find that you can actually turn a profit relatively easily.

The rental rate for your property will be dependent on several factors—where is it? What is the neighborhood like? How is the school line? What are the local amenities? The amenities in the house? All of this is important to consider, along with how many rooms, the quality of the home itself, and more. You must make sure that you are asking a reasonable amount for the property that you are renting.

Should I Bother with Rentals out of My Area?

Some people think that they would be better off buying a property that is further away. They choose to do so usually because they find somewhere that has really low market values for housing compared to where they are, and they choose to latch onto it, seeing it as an investment property. After all, one thing is usually true about real estate—the property, when maintained, will grow easily. When it comes to making money, then getting the units that have the highest return on investment potential is one of the best ways to make money. If you live somewhere with a very high cost of living, buying a house in rural South Carolina for a fraction of the price can seem like a fantastic deal. However, as a beginner, you want to consider purchasing closer to home. You want to do this so you can have an easier time dealing with the property. If you want to utilize out-of-state investments, you want to first get used to it locally first. Try to aim for close to home, or at the very least, within a reasonable distance, from where you live. It should be easily drivable without becoming a major hassle.

How Long Will it Take to Profit?

Of course, you probably want to know how quickly you can turn a profit on your investment as well. After all, we usually find ourselves thinking of the money that it would cost to get started, and it can seem daunting to purchase a house if you are not profiting almost immediately. Of course, however, you must remember that in real estate investments, usually slow and steady will win the race. You must start small and recognize that it will take a few months before you really start to see big returns. Your biggest return when it comes to real estate investing is usually found in being able to make money through the appreciation of the value of your property. However, be patient. All sorts of factors could cause you to have to spend longer waiting for the funds to be there for you.

How Can I Maximize My Profit Margins?

You are also probably curious about maximizing your profits as well. This makes sense from an investor's standpoint—you want to be certain that you make as much money as possible. When it comes to maximizing those margins, there are even a few ways that are quite simple to tap into. Though ultimately, market value will matter immensely, you should also consider the fact that you can make a significant profit just by paying attention to what you are doing and being smart. Consider these simple changes to ensure that you can increase the profit margins on your property:

- Keep your property pricing competitive
- Make sure that all tenants are screened to minimize the risk to your property or to losing money to unpaid rent
- Make additional services available in your home for a fee. For example, use luxury appliances, hardwood, and granite counters to up the value of the home.
- Maintain your property well to ensure that it is in tip-top condition so that you can skip the expensive repairs later on.
- Upgrade through renovations if necessary to make the property more modern.

Should I Hire a Property Manager?

Finally, many people ask themselves if they should hire property managers to work on their property. This is something that is highly dependent upon the goals that you have for yourself and how much work you want to do or avoid. Depending upon what you want to do with yourself, you might want to pay for the property manager, but if you are okay putting in the work while also pocketing more money, then hiring a property manager would be a good option for you. This is really a choice that you will have to make for yourself to figure out what you want and just how compatible your goals are with what you are doing.

Chapter 2: Ten Secrets to Avoid Making a Mistake in the Real Estate Market

With those simple questions answered, you should have a better idea of the concept of investing in the real estate market. Now, you must figure out if this is something that you really want to do. It is not as intimidating as it might seem at first. If you include some key actions, you can actually avoid making several common mistakes to help yourself be successful in the real estate market. There are several potential mistakes that can be made if you do not know what you are doing or how to regulate yourself, and because of that, it is often a good idea to pay attention to the tried and true tips and tricks that will help you avoid those basic beginner's mistakes.

In this chapter, we are going to look at the ten secrets that you can use to help yourself profit better. If you want to make sure that you have as much money in your pocket as possible, this chapter is for you—it will help you to ensure that you do get that money effectively. All you have to do is ensure that you are on the right track and ensure that you can begin profiting. Let's take a look at those ten secrets now.

Don't Waste Money Trying to Learn—Use Free Resources

A common mistake that people make is that they tend to spend a bunch of money on classes and resources, thinking that the resources and the option will actually make them a better investor or help them to be more successful, but they actually completely miss out on what they should be doing. This is a huge problem in many contexts, and if you are not smart, you will waste money that could have otherwise gone to boost your investments rather than being wasted on books that will never be taken off of the bookshelf or with classes that you will not really pay much attention through.

One of the best things that you can do to avoid this mistake is to make use of free resources that are available to you. Free and low-cost resources, from books like this one to finding information on the internet through your own personal studies, can help you immensely with figuring out how to make the money that you are looking for. The internet is wide and vast at this point, and you do not need to feel like you have to spend the money on classes when you can just as easily freely learn about the investment for yourself. When you avoid wasting money, you then have it available to yourself for future use. It becomes something that you can utilize with ease, and all you have to do is make sure that you can take care of it.

Don't Skip the Basics

Of course, just because you shouldn't waste money on classes that you do not need doesn't mean that you should skip out on the basics. You want to make money somehow, and the best way to do so is often by making use of these other free options to help you learn. It is important for you to know what you are doing so you do not waste time or money. By understanding the ins and outs of real estate investments, you should be able to make use of it. You should be able to find ways that you can learn the basics without blowing the money either. Finding that great middle ground is what will help you. If you do not know the basics of how to invest, then you are going to get yourself into financial difficulty, and that can be a major problem or even kill your ability to make money in the first place.

Don't Let Fear Rule You

When you are investing thousands or hundreds of thousands of dollars, it can be easy to be intimidated. It can be difficult for you to feel like you are able to properly making the right choice when you look at something that could very easily send you into financial ruin. However, remember that there is no true reward without some degree of risk either. If you do not put out the risks, then you will risk suffering the consequences of your failures. If you allow for fear to rule over you, you will start to miss out on options that could have been good for you. If you are not careful, you can run into situations in which you cannot make money because you were too afraid to act. Your fear should be there, and some degree of fear is normal and even healthy, but you also cannot let your fear control everything that you do. You must make sure that you find that nice, common middle ground in which you know what you are doing, and you do it well. Remember to trust yourself, especially if you have been making good financial decisions, and you have taught yourself the basics thoroughly to ensure that you would be safe to do whatever you set out to do.

Don't Choose the First Property

Make sure that when you go out to start looking at properties, you do not choose out the first one that you see. You want to make sure that you look at more than one and really weigh your options before you put down an offer. Don't fall in love with something at first sight. Many people tend to fall into this trap of buying the first thing on the market without really considering how they could have followed up with it. They do not think about the implications of doing what they do until they have already locked themselves into a contract, and they realize that they made a major mistake simply by not realizing that there would be potentially better properties later on. You should never simply be willing to accept the first property without seeing others to compare it to.

Don't Get Stuck in the Idea of Waiting for a Better Deal

Conversely, you must remember not to get yourself stuck in the idea that there is something better coming later on as well. Yes, there probably will be something better in the future, but if all you do is consistently wonder about what you can get that is better in the future, how are you ever going to actually make that money for yourself? How are you ever going to say that enough is enough, and you are ready to make your investment? If you are constantly waiting around for the best possible deal, then you are going to spend an awful lot of time wondering about what you can get later on. You will spend a lot of time wishing for something more without ever actually getting it. This can be a major problem for you—you must make sure that you do actually choose something.

You want to make sure that at some point, you bite the bullet and take one of the available options, even if it is not absolutely perfect in every way or if you think that something better will come later. You will not make money if you are not actively investing, and that means that you can run into all sorts of problems. You must make sure that you do properly push yourself at some point to buy.

Don't Think that Real Estate Investment is for the Wealthy

A common mistake that people make is believing that real estate investing is only for the wealthy. They never even consider it because they assume that there is no reason for them to invest in the first place. However, this is a major problem—if you do this, you run into an issue with never actually investing. If you never go out of your way to make an investment, how are you ever going to actually profit? There is no reason that you should get stuck in this idea that real estate investing is only for the wealthy—anyone can do it, and it does not have to be very expensive either. It also isn't something that is incredibly difficult. Yes, there is a learning curve, but that does not mean that you should not try for it. You must make sure that you are taking the time to get what you want, and that means being willing to, at the very least, try.

Remember, there are ways that you can invest in properties without needing half of a million dollars to put down on the house. You can actually invest even with much smaller numbers, meaning that there is no reason that you should get stuck in this idea that there is no way for you to make that money or profit in the first place. You can do it—you just have to know what you are doing.

Don't Fall in Love

Additionally, it is strongly recommended that you do not fall in love with property along the way. If you start dipping your feet into this process, eventually, you will find that you can actually fall in love with either your tenants or with your property. You can get too attached to the property itself, no longer seeing it as so much of an investment as something that ought to be protected or defended. If you are not careful, you can run into significant problems with this—you could, for example, fool yourself into thinking that you should sell off the property, so you do not have to run the risk of losing money, or you could also choose to invest too much into the interior, but realizing that you lose money because you can only charge a certain amount before you run into trouble.

When you start to get too close to the tenants, you can run into other issues as well—you can find yourself struggling to set or maintain boundaries, and as a result, you end up stuck. You end up in a position in which you end up losing out on money because you would rather be nice to your current tenant. Blurring that professional line can actually cost you money in the long run. Be mindful of this.

Instead, leave emotion out of the entire process. There is no reason that you should allow yourself to get so worked up over everything. Rather, you should focus instead about the cold logic and the numbers behind it. This is strictly business- keep it that way.

Don't Skip the Planning

Oftentimes, people choose to skip the planning stage. They realize that they set out to do something or to purchase a property to invest, and then they realize that they have no idea what they are doing. They could find themselves wishing they knew—but their financial goals are so unclear that they are actually losing money instead. You must be fully aware of the money that you bring in, but you also must be well aware of your financial goals as well. You want to make sure that you understand what you expect to get out of your investments—and then you must make it a point to figure out how to get that. If you play your cards just right, you can ensure that you get everything just right. You can make sure that ultimately, you choose everything out accordingly, and as a result, you end up ahead. However, if you lack that planning, you will struggle to meet those goals.

Don't Purchase from Unmotivated Sellers

One mistake that can be made is attempting to purchase something from someone that clearly does not want to sell. It can seem like you can buy things from others by making off-market offers and hoping that someone decides to go for it, but you could also discover that the unmotivated seller will likely up the cost significantly. They may operate on the idea that everything is for sale if the price is right, and that can be highly problematic if you do not know what you are doing.

This is a great way that you can start to lose out on money just by virtue of the fact that you did not pay close enough attention to what was going on. If you want to do better, you can usually get better prices by buying from people who actually *are* motivated to sell. By sticking to on the market units and properties, you can usually find that you are much more likely to successfully get the prices that are within the range that you are willing to buy for. You do not have to break the bank for a perfect property when you are only using it for investments.

Don't Expect Immediate Results

When it comes to making money, you probably want to ensure that you are making money as soon as possible. However, investments take time to really bring that return back to you. It will take time for you to start profiting from your ventures and you must be realistic about your expectations. You cannot assume that your results will allow for you to make money immediately—you must turn it around and see that ultimately, you can make money on your investments with ease. Ultimately, being able to do this is highly desired—but also quite unreliable. You cannot hope to make that kind of money immediately in any legitimate fashion. If you want to make money, you must be patient. Wait it out. You will most likely make money, but it takes time, effort, hard work, knowing what you are doing, and a little bit of luck before you can get it just right. If you want to do it, you can—but you will find that it will require you to take time.

Chapter 3: Investing in Real Estate as a Beginner

Now we get into the good stuff. Now is where we start to look at what it is going to take you to be able to invest in real estate as a beginner. This is something that many people hope to learn—but it will take time. This guide is here to help you start your investment process—remember that this is just one of many different strategy guides, and you can expect there to be many other options out there as well.

Real estate investing is a fantastic option that you can use to boost up your portfolio so you can achieve that financial independence that you want over time. Remember, the best investment portfolios are those that have income coming from several different directions—you want to be able to draw from them as quickly as possible. Though the barrier of entry feels large, it is not as bad as you probably think—it is something that you can do with ease. All you have to do is ensure that you know what you are doing, and even if you do not have much money, you can begin to invest.

Within this chapter, you are going to see a general guide to real estate investing. We will take the time to consider the various types of investments, how to make money, how to actively and passively invest, and how to invest without money. This will help you to get started on the right foot, investing properly without much of a problem. If you want to know how to invest in real estate, this will be your comprehensive guide to doing just that.

What Types of Real Estate Investments Are There?

All things considered, you have four different options when you decide to invest in real estate. Though there are several different strategies that you can use, ultimately, you will be utilizing one of four key types of investments. These are residential, commercial, industrial, and land. Each of these four options is slightly different.

However, most beginners focus on either residential or commercial investments for their first ventures.

Residential real estate

Residential real estate is that within which people reside. If you can live in the building, it is a type of residential real estate. This means that you would be encompassing houses, duplexes, townhomes, mobile homes, and apartments. This also represents one of the most common forms of investing that there is. Most often, people purchase either a single or multifamily home and then rent it out to get that passive income. Of course, there is still upkeep that needs to be considered here as well—but you will be able to choose just how active of a role you want in all of that and for those who simply want to own the property without much of an obligation to do anything else, they pay a management company to take care of everything for them in their name. Then, all those owners have to do is fund it.

Commercial real estate

Commercial real estate refers to businesses or apartments when the apartments have more than four units within them. This is how you would invest in shops, restaurants, or other buildings that do not count as residences. Keep in mind that any apartment complexes with four or more units will always be deemed commercial real estate. Less than four would be deemed residential. Typically, people stick to residential because it is less strictly regulated. When you want to invest in commercial real estate, you must worry about tax regulations and city codes as well.

Industrial real estate

Industrial real estate is similar to commercial real estate but on a much larger scale. Here, you are looking at investing in power plants, factories, or warehouses. This is usually not common for first-time investors—the price point is quite inhibitive, and it is far more complicated to manage than the other kinds of real estate that are available to you.

Land real estate

Land real estate is, as it implies, a way to invest that involves simply purchasing land. It is one of the easiest ways that you can invest— all you do is purchase a plot of land that is not yet developed. You can then either sit on the land, or you can flip it if you got it at a good deal. You could also rent it out if you wanted to. There are many different options here, depending upon what you want to do and how you choose to go about it.

What should I choose?

If you are starting out, it is generally recommended that you start out with residential real estate and then work your way up. If you know what you are doing, you can start to make plenty of money. Once you know the rules and codes that you will need with residential real estate, you can start moving on to the commercial real estate. It has a steeper learning curve, but you can do well if you know what you are doing. No matter how you start, however, it is strongly recommended that you start out with becoming competent in one before moving on to the next. Typically, people start with residential due to the fact that it is often cheaper and will be easier to master.

How Do I Start Making Money?

The next question that everyone asks is how the money in real estate is made. The truth is, it is made quite easily. There are three primary ways that you can make money in real estate, and any of them would provide you with great benefits. You can make money through appreciation, rent, or interest. Each of these different types of earning work differently.

Appreciation refers to the value of the property growing and developing, so you can then sell it at a price that is higher than what you paid when you bought it. When you build up money this way, you are making your profit through the value that the property increases by. However, this is also a very high-risk endeavor—you have no guarantee that you will be able to sell at more than you paid.

Rent is another way to build equity through which you are able to build profit through an income. You will be charging someone to live in that property or to use that property, and as you do so, you will be gaining money through the fact that you will be getting those monthly payments in return for usage of the land. This is another great way to profit—but again, it is somewhat risky. You only see your profit-building if you have someone that is going to actively pay back what they use of your property. If they don't, then you have other issues. This is precisely why it is so important for you to screen your renters accordingly to ensure that you do not run into those kinds of issues.

Interest can be built up as well if you provide loans. In these situations, you usually provide money, and a real estate developer will take care of everything else. This is perfect for investments that are low on time. You do not get as much money in return, but you also build up interest, little by little, over time, much like how a bank does when they loan you money. Usually, this works somewhat like a mortgage—they pay you back a certain amount monthly with interest while you lend them money.

Flipping vs. holding properties

If you are going to be trying to build appreciation, you are going to utilize one of two methods to build that money up and turn a profit. You will either flip it, or you will buy it and hold it. Each of these are quite valid ways that you can make money in their own rights—you just have to determine which is the right way for you.

Flipping is much more hands-on—when you flip a property, you will purchase a property, then do some minor fixes to it before selling it, attempting to flip it as quickly as possible. You will be able to make a quick buck this way, but you also are putting sweat equity into it- you are fixing it up to get more value out of the property. This works well, but it is hands-on. This is typically what you see happen if you buy a "fixer-upper"—a house that will require extensive work to make it respectable, or in some cases, even habitable. If you can contract this work out at a low enough price or you can do it yourself, you can make money quickly.

Some people, however, prefer to hold properties and wait for them to appreciate nature. If you have ever looked at the housing market, you see that over time, the value of houses goes up. This, however, requires you to speculate—you have to look at the market, predict how it will go, and purchase at just the right time. If you do this the right way, you can usually make some money. Because waiting for a property to build value on its own takes time, people often buy a property, rent it out for a while, and then sell it to flip it later to make a profit.

Active Investing

Active investing is much more hands-on than other options. When you use active investing, you are usually going to be involved with the process. The good thing about active investing is that you see how your money is being spent. You see what it does and how far it goes. You get to make those important decisions that will help you to properly begin to see what is going on at any point in time. If you actively invest in your property, you will be able to see how it is working. You also tend to make more money when you are actively involved in the day-to-day work of the maintenance of what you are doing.

There are several different types of active investments that you can make. The most popular out there is house flipping and being the landlord of your own rental property. These two methods allow you to make that money and maintain it long-term. Because active investing allows you to make more money just due to the fact that you do not have to outsource work that would otherwise need to be done in your stead, it is a common and popular choice for beginners that are not quite sure what they are doing. Because beginners do not always have a lot of money, they find that easy DIY fixes, such as putting in new tile or doing some general landscaping is a great way to add value to the property.

House flipping is one option that has high-profit potential, especially if you know what you are doing or if you have connections with people that can give you good rates on whatever work may need to be finished. If you know what you are doing, you can properly turn decent profits. However, this is a relatively high risk—you can run into unanticipated expenses, and you also may have the struggle to sell off the property as well. If you cannot manage this well, you could very well lose money instead of making it.

If you are the landlord of a rental property, you will also be able to make decent money—but you still have some concerns that you will have to address. As the landlord, you must maintain the property. You will be responsible for all day-to-day operations, and you will need to have enough of a sinking fund for the property to handle any unintended expenses. If the roof fails, you must have the money to fix it. If the tenants break something, you will need to be able to provide the funds to fix it. And, if the tenants manage to completely trash the place if you kick them out, as some unruly, frustrated tenants may do when evicted out of sheer spite, you will need to be able to pay for any unexpected expenses. It might not be something that you want to have to do—but as a landlord, you are effectively ensuring that their house is kept to code, and you will need to do so to a higher degree than you would probably do to your own home. You will need to make sure that your property meets certain tenant rules, and in some cases, you will only have a couple of days to respond to fix necessities. This will be largely dependent upon the state that you live in, with states like Washington giving landlords 24 hours to restore heat, water, electricity, or any imminent hazards. You will have 72 hours to repair primary appliances such as the fridge, range, or oven, or if there are plumbing problems. Anything else must be repaired in 10 days. If you do not, there are potential legal ramifications that you will have to face.

Passive Investing

Passive investing is a bit different than active. In passive investing, you spend less time and have less stress, but you also will find that you have many other things to consider as well. As a passive investor, you are giving up some of your earnings in return for your time or sanity. You might think that the processes are not worth the added expense of a management company. Many people who are busy and still want to invest without the worries enjoy the passive forms of real estate. This will keep you from having to get up at 3 am when the heating stops working in the dead of winter or if something catastrophic goes wrong completely randomly when you least expect it. That will be the responsibility of your management team, and you will be free to enjoy your sleep without interruption. This is perfect for you—if you want to be able to get the benefits without the difficult parts, then you can do so with ease. Of course, you will also get a smaller return as well. The two primary passive forms of investing involve REITs and turnkey rentals.

REITs stands for a real estate investment trust. This is a trust that owns thousands of other investment properties. When you choose to invest in a REIT, you are investing in a company. You provide money to the company, which then takes that money and invests that money to turn a profit—and they pay you in return. This is the real estate equivalent of utilizing mutual funds in the stock market—you invest and have someone else handle all of the hard work for you. It pays dividends in return—usually, 90% of taxable income must be returned to the shareholder. The amount that you get may vary, but you will see regular dividend payouts as well. The key here is that you may not have as considerable returns as you might see with other methods—but you will also be investing in a much safer way as well.

Turnkey rentals allow you to purchase a property that is already filled up with a renter. Companies specializing in turnkeys would take care of it all for you—they will find you that home that already has renters, and then they negotiate everything for you. Because the companies do not own the homes, you do not have to worry about being negotiated with to make you purchase a property that is not as good as it could be. These types of all-in-one companies will provide great investment options for those who do not want to deal with anything. You simply give you the money, and they will do it all. You won't even have to find a management company.

Risk Tolerance

Now, you must understand just how risk-tolerant you are before you begin. The more risk that you take, the more reward you are likely to get—your potential reward goes up along with risk. However, that can be difficult to manage. At what point do you draw the line? At what point do you tell yourself that you would rather have less return to avoid the risk? For people who want to avoid risk, they do lessen the return on investment. However, that will be something for you to determine. It is up to you to figure out just how risky you want to be with your money. If you do not mind the risk, then great—you can make more money. If you need safer, regular pay, however, you have that as an option as well. All you have to do is ensure that you figure that out for yourself.

Investing without Money

If you do not have money, you can still make money in other ways. You do not have to have a massive amount of cash in the bank or burning a hole in your pocket—you can make money by being the middle man. This takes time, effort, and having the right connections, but if you manage to be the finder for the real estate agent, you can actually make money that way as well. Those finders fees can start allowing you to get that additional money to invest in other ways as well.

This is as simple as connecting buyers to agents or to connect properties to buyers. When you do this, sort of playing real estate matchmaker, you can actually make a decent amount of money that you can utilize. It might not be as lucrative as, say, flipping a property, but you are still making money.

Chapter 4: Why Should I Invest?

Now, with all of that written out for you, you might still be wondering if real estate investment is right for you. The truth is, that is something you must choose for yourself. However, one thing is certain: There are many reasons that you should. Consider this chapter the list of reasons that your real estate investment is a good one to make. Remember that, as you go over this, these are the perks of having a good, regular investment property.

Cash Flow

Cash flow is one of the most compelling perks of being able to invest in the real estate market. When you invest in real estate, you will see cash flow somehow. Whether in rental payments or through simply profiting from a quick real estate flip, you have options here that will help you to make money on your investments. If you make a good, well-thought-out investment, you should see cash flow relatively quickly. In many cases as well, you will see that the money that you make only goes up over time rather than down. As you make money, you should see that as your mortgage is paid down, your equity on your property builds, especially as the value of your property goes up as well due to inflation, and that allows you to make even more money.

Tax Deductions and Breaks

Many investors love the different advantageous tax breaks that can be earned through real estate. This is especially true if you are renting out residential areas—if you rent out a home, there are certain expenses that you pay that can all be deducted from your taxes, helping to whittle away at your liability over time. This is perfect if you are worried about how much you might owe at tax time each year. Generally speaking, if you are managing a rental, you can deduct reasonable amounts of your expenditure.

Appreciation

Another reason that investors flock to real estate is recognizing that there is appreciation. Because the values of your property will go up over time as long as you own in a desirable area and you have the right amount of maintenance and upkeep, you can actually see the value skyrocket. A nice house in a good school district in a nice area of town can appreciate rapidly and start building wealth for you. That appreciation goes right toward the equity that you have- your mortgage does not grow with it, but the value of the property does. This means that if you buy a house with a $250,000 mortgage and five years later, that property is worth $375,000 just due to inflation, you have profited.

Building Equity and Wealth

As you pay down mortgages on properties, you start to build up equity, which counts as part of your net worth. As equity builds, you start to gain more leverage for future properties, allowing you to build up even more. It is the perfect cycle that will continue and sustain itself—your equity will build wealth, and with your wealth, you can afford more equity. The more properties that you are able to invest in, the more money that you will have overall, and that is a huge perk.

Diversifying your Portfolio

When you invest, you have an investment portfolio. Within it, you may have some stocks, some retirement accounts, or even some precious metals. Another method of investment that is included in that portfolio is, you guessed it—real estate. Through investing in real estate, you start to build up that portfolio as well, diversifying it.

One thing that just about any financial advisor will tell you is that the best portfolios are those that are highly diversified. The most diverse portfolios are going to be the most durable—they will be able to get through any crashes that might happen. The stock market might drop, but if you also have money in precious metals, you might see them go up. Likewise, you may see your real estate hold steady in the drop of the market. Having that diverse portfolio is absolutely essential if you want to make sure that you have that money secure where you need it. It is strongly recommended that you diversify your portfolio and real estate actually has some particular advantages.

In particular, real estate tends to have a negative correlation with many of the other assets that are out there. The stock market might start to dip, but that could actually help to propel the real estate market up as well. This means that it is a great way to hedge against any sort of financial problems that could come with economic crashes.

Real Estate Leverage

Another consideration to make when it comes to investing is the fact that you can utilize leverage. Leverage refers to the utilization of lending money and creating debt to increase a return on investment. For example, consider that a 20% investment for a mortgage on a house will buy you the house that you want—this is leverage. The property effectively serves as collateral for it. The property serves as collateral for loans that may be given out, and that allows for easier financing. If you wanted to provide the financing for a property, you would have that leverage there—the loan would be secured by virtue of having that collateral on the table if you needed to tap into it.

Compare this to lending money for a project that had no leverage attached to it. You would have nothing to take back if the other party chose to default on the terms of the loans. If you run into this problem, you could see all sorts of issues, and that could be a major problem for you. To reclaim your funds, you would have to go through alternative methods such as through the court to sue for it—but you would have no guarantee that you would get the money back. After all, you cannot get something when there is nothing from someone. This is why real estate is a better option—it is a relatively safe investment that will help you to avoid problems if you are lending for loans.

Competitive Returns

Yes, there is risk involved in real estate, but for the most part, it is actually the case that you will see better average returns than if you were to invest in the stock market. The risk might be higher, but the return is often worth it if you are smart with your money, and you make good, safe decisions on how to invest. This is a great way for you to protect yourself while still profiting. If you want to make the most out of your investments, you should be able to get a good deal of money relative to risk through these types of investments. They are great for people and can strongly help you.

Inflation Hedge

Real estate is actually able to hedge against inflation as well—this means that as inflation goes up, it does not lose its value. While inflation causes the value of the dollar to drop, housing rarely suffers from this—in fact, real estate tends to gain value over time rather than losing it. This makes real estate a fantastic way to hedge against inflation. While the rental rates that you charge may go up with inflation and the value of your house will increase as well, your mortgage will stay the same. This means that over time, your mortgage will be significantly lower than what you could get for the property, and that means that you make more money as well. This is a great way that you can make money with ease. You literally just have to sit on the property and it hedges against inflation for you. If you want your wealth to retain value instead of losing it, this will help you with that.

REITs

Finally, one of the most compelling reasons that you should invest in real estate is the utilization of REITs. Remember, these will give you a way to invest without having to jump straight in. It is perfect if you want to get started with little risk. Through buying and selling

REITs, you can actually make money quickly. They also usually offer higher dividends than you would see from other stocks for a similar rate of investment. This means that if you want to make money relatively quickly, this is a safe and easy way to do so without requiring a massive amount of work on your part.

Ultimately, there are many compelling reasons that you should choose real estate as a primary point of investment for yourself and your own wealth. All things considered, it does allow you to make money relatively easily—but you also must deal with certain risks, and at some point, you must be able to tell yourself what enough is, so you stop running into these problems over and over again. If you want to make that money, you can do so. Remember, don't let your own insecurities and fears keep you from making that profit that you were destined to make. You can do it! But remember, you can only receive it if you first give. You must start out with investing so you can then begin to make money as well. You will have to take that first risk if you want to hope to profit.

Chapter 5: Making Money with the Least Amount of Risk

Investing is scary. It can be terrifying to put your money somewhere and not knowing what will happen next. When it comes to being able to invest, you want to know what you can do to avoid or minimize risk as much as possible. When you are ready to invest, especially as a beginner, you might find that you are much more concerned about losing money than an avid investor who may not be so concerned about how much money is going into something. This is because when you have just started investing, you likely have less money than someone who has been investing for a longer period of time. Of course, you're worried about minimizing risk. Of course, you're worried about what will happen if you lose that money.

Minimizing the amount of money that you lose becomes critical. Being able to ensure that you protect that money will help you to keep afloat. The end goal of the investment is to make more money, and that money is only made through successfully navigating through those difficult and sometimes turbulent waters. The problem with investments is that they are not guaranteed. There is no way for you to be certain that you'd make money. There is no way for you to be certain that your investment won't turn around and cost you a massive amount in lost funds.

Of course, being able to do so is not always easy. It can be hard to figure out what to do and how to make it work, but when you do, you can start cutting down on the risk. When it comes to figuring out how to limit risk, the best way to do so is by making sure that you pay close attention to the ways in which you should be investing. There are certain kinds of investments that are simply better—they are less risky than others, and that matters immensely. You can minimize risk by making sure that you're utilizing certain kinds of properties or tendencies.

Within this chapter, we are going to go over what you can do to begin reducing risk so you can be certain that you are on the right track. We are going to consider what it will take for you to figure out how to cut that risk by using rental properties. We will discuss how rental properties can cut the amount of risk, as well as how you can use the buy and hold method. We will go over REITs as a low-risk option, and finally, we will take a look at how to diversify a portfolio to ensure that you do cut down the risk.

Long-Term Rental Properties

Rental properties, despite coming with some risks, can be some of the safest forms of investments you can make, especially when you compare them to methods such as stock market investments. This is because housing is always in demand. Someone always needs a property to live in. We all need to have some sort of shelter, especially living in areas where the climate may be less than favorable. This means that if you have a good property, you are going to see a decent return. Think about it—if you have a property in a good spot, you are going to have a tenant basically constantly. If you have someone in your unit, you are going to turn a profit regularly. Rental properties, especially if you get a good tenant, you will be able to get a good turnaround.

This is because there is a huge demand for rental properties. The current market is not large enough to suit the number of people looking for houses. There are also people who may want to rent a house over an apartment just because it works better for them. This is important for you to take advantage of as well. There will almost always be a demand for housing, especially if you plan it out well. If you make sure that you are investing in a property in a place where the schools are good and there are plenty of family-oriented things to do, you can probably find that you can have a renter for several years before they move on. Before people buy their first homes, they usually rent for a while.

Of course, there are some risks involved here. When it comes to renting out a property to others, you have to be prepared for what will happen if people do not treat your property respectfully. You must be smart about who you choose to rent to. You need to take the time to screen your tenants to ensure that you are not making a risky choice that is going to backfire on you or cause you significant issues later on. For example, making sure that the renter has not had a bankruptcy or is able to verify making enough money to properly afford the property is a great way that you can cut down the risk of long-term rentals.

Many people have fantastic luck with this option—they are able to make plenty of income just by renting out their property. Of course, this is not without a significant amount of investment, both financially and otherwise. You must be able to pay attention to your property and have the funds to make sure that your property is maintained. If you can do this, you should be able to find that your property is actually going to make you a significant amount of money.

Short-Term Rental Properties

Another relatively low-risk option for real estate investment is jumping on the short-term rental bandwagon. This is renting out properties on Airbnb and the like to allow for people to come in and pay per night or per week or other short-term periods of time in your home. Usually, there is no lease, and there is no real expectation of tenancy that you would see in a long-term rental. This can be highly lucrative, especially if you live in the right area to make this work for you. However, you can further cut the risks by paying attention to the area that you have chosen to rent in and make sure that you have done your research. Especially if you live in a touristy area, you are going to have no shortage of turnover in your living quarters that you can make use of.

Buy and Hold Real Estate

While some investors choose to play the flipping game, in which they purchase a property and immediately after flip it to make a profit, you can actually reduce your risk if you were to purchase and hold a property. This is perfect for regions where the real estate market is currently holding steady and where properties are appreciating. When you do this, you allow the property that you have purchased to simply grow in value. Take some of the hottest real estate markets in the nation right now—if you were to look at Tacoma, Washington, one of the quickest-growing markets in the nation at the moment, you could purchase a three-bedroom, two bath house with 1200 square feet for roughly $350,000. According to forecasts on the housing market, that same house was worth just $228,000 in 2016. This means that if you had purchased this property in 2016 and allowed it to grow, you would have made $122,000 over the course of 4 years just by holding the property. How much is that per month? That is a growth of $2,541.67/month in the value of the property.

Now, many times, people choose to rent out the properties that they are holding as well. This can significantly boost the amount of income that you get, building that cash flow while you intended to hold the property as well. That very same house in Tacoma may rent for nearly $2000 per month as well. This means that if you played your cards right, your home would be growing in value of roughly $2500/month, and you would also bring in $2000/month as well through rental income.

Real Estate Investment Trusts

REITs offer another form of safe, low-risk investments that can help you to ensure that your money is going where it should be. By making sure that you invest in REITs, you will be able to ensure that your money stays secure because you won't be worrying about the property that is being invested in—you are simply investing in the company itself. The key difference there changes everything—it protects you and your investment from problems that landlords may open themselves up to.

Because REITs are companies that finance real estate ventures, they are usually a bit more secure—they are usually established enough that when one or two properties run into issues, they are able to fix the problem and get by without much of a problem. Many investors prefer this method because of the fact that they are more guaranteed. While you may not make as much money using REITs as you would if you owned the properties themselves, you will still be profiting.

Diversification

Finally, one of the best ways that you can benefit from making money is by diversifying your funds. If you know what you are doing, you can ensure that your entire portfolio is going to be more secure than it otherwise would be. Think about it this way—if you diversify your real estate investment portfolio, meaning that you have several different options that you use for your investments, you are protecting yourself. You are creating several different fail-safes that can protect you and your assets from the funds that you are going to be using. By making sure that you've got all of these funds all protected, you can guarantee that you are on the right track, making certain that you can hedge against any problems that you may encounter. If you have all of your eggs in one basket, dropping that basket or having that basket fail becomes catastrophic. Because of that, you want to focus on the fact that you can do better. You want to put more of your eggs in several different baskets, spreading them out instead. When you do that, you can make sure that you do defend yourself from the problem. You want to ensure that you've taken the time to diversify to prevent that basket from shattering all of your eggs in one go.

When it comes to diversifying your portfolio, you want to ensure that you look at several options that you have. Diversifying is something that can happen with all sorts of different methods. You could, for example, purchase a house and then hold it while renting it out at the same time. As you do this, you may choose to push your income from your rent to invest in REITs as well. This allows you to begin investing more. Over time, you may choose to get some commercial properties and other properties as well. This is a great way for you to really diversify that portfolio.

Lowering Risks

When it comes to cutting down your chances of having problems, thankfully, there are several options that you have that can help. If you want to ensure that you are keeping your risk as low as possible, some of the best starting points involve making sure that you know what *not* to do. Yes, there are things that you should never do if you want to lower your risks. Now, as you read through this, you will probably find yourself wondering why these would be listed as things to avoid when many people may do well using them. Take house flipping, for example—it has been glorified on television. It has been made out to be some sort of magical way that you can make a quick buck if you are just a bit handy ad willing to go out of your way to make money work. But, the problem with this is that if you do so, you are going to open yourself up to all sorts of serious risks that could destroy you if you don't know how to manage them. You need to make sure that you do pay attention to what you can do to lower and mitigate those risks so you can be certain that at the end of the day, you are safe. You want to ensure that you are taking the time to reduce risks where you can so you can feel like ultimately, you are making the right choice for you.

Now, let's take a look at some of the biggest things to avoid.

Avoid flipping houses

When it comes to real estate, you must ensure that you avoid flipping houses. The more that you do this, the better. Yes, you can make a pretty penny by doing so if you get lucky—but you may also end up spending far more than you meant to. If you are new to investing, or if you do not have large amounts of free money that you can use, you may find that this will simply leave you vulnerable and cause problems for you rather than grant you the value that you are looking for. This can especially be the case if you find out that there is something else wrong with the property that you were unaware of at first. Or, it could be the case that when you attempt to do sell, it takes so much longer than you initially thought. This can be problematic for you as well if you do not know what you are doing. If you cannot manage everything the right way, you can run into serious trouble. If you want low-risk investments, this is not the way to go.

Avoid speculation

Likewise, you will want to avoid speculation. Yes, real estate is attractive due to the way that it works, but it is also problematic in many ways for people as well. If you have not been careful about how you need to do something, then you may find yourself suffering. Speculation without knowing what you are doing and without being able to eat the loss if you speculated the wrong way is no good for you—you must make sure that you take a different approach to the situation to make sure that you are on the right track. Speculation should be left to the experts—just avoid the risk altogether.

Run the math

When it comes to lowering the risk, you must make sure that you do the math the right way. This means making sure that you've chosen a property that is worthwhile before putting your money into it and making sure that you do your due diligence and ensure that you are working the right way. Make sure that you work to find low-risk, high-yield investments by being highly selective about what you are choosing to do. If you know what you are doing and you do it the right way, you can ensure that ultimately, you are making the right choice. This is done by running analysis calculators, by looking at what the anticipated return on investment will be, and more. By doing this, you can work to make sure that your investment's potential lives up to what you need it to.

Find good tenants

This should go without saying, but make sure that ultimately, you are going to find good tenants for yourself. If you want to ensure that you are profiting, you will need to make sure that you are selective about who you rent to. When you do this, you will ensure that you are saving cash. When you do this the right way, you can ensure that you are profiting. When it comes to making sure that you are profiting the right way, the best way is to get a tenant that is going to continue to rent the unit consistently. This will help you to keep that influx of cash coming in, especially because, as a landlord, you are, to a certain extent, at the mercy of your renter. If your renter doesn't pay rent willingly, you have to go out of your way to get it through legal methods, and that can take a lot of time and effort. If you have to do this, you might find that you lose more money. This is why it is so imperative to work on screening your tenants carefully. When you do, you guarantee that your own personal assets are protected and that matters immensely.

Have backup plans

Finally, make sure that you always have contingency plans. When you are investing, you always need a damage control plan that you can use to help protect yourself. You may want to ensure that you know what you can do to protect yourself and your investments. It could be that you choose to figure out what you will do if something goes wrong. It could be having money set aside in case of a catastrophic failure or otherwise. When you have that backup plan, you will be able to protect your investment more.

Chapter 6: Evaluating Properties

So, you've decided that you want to purchase a property. Great! You've made a huge step toward what you need to do. You've chosen to do something that will help you successfully invest your funds, and that is a wonderful decision. But, before you do anything, you might realize that you don't know how to choose a property. Choosing out what you intend to purchase can be difficult—it can be hard to figure out what it is that you should be looking for. But, the truth is, you can figure out how best to do so if you learn what you should be looking for. After all, if you choose a poor property, you are not likely to actually get that return on investment that you were looking for, and obviously, that is not what you want.

Thankfully, however, you can get a guide that can help you to figure out how to purchase. You can learn to evaluate what makes a good investment all by making sure that you know what you are looking at. Learning to choose good properties will help you to ensure that your property that you have chosen will actually be highly successful. We will first look at what makes for a desirable rental property, evaluating those that are meant to be utilized for living within. These rental properties can usually provide a decent chunk of change just through investing properly, and if you get lucky and happen to get the property just right, you could stumble upon what becomes a cash cow. Then, we will also address what you can do to profit from a commercial property as well.

Learning to evaluate the properties that you will purchase helps you to ensure that you do not unintentionally wind up, causing problems for yourself. It helps you to weigh the pros and cons so you can figure out which properties are going to provide the best return on investment for you and if you can do this successfully, you will discover that ultimately, you can invest well.

Features of a Profitable Rental Property

When it comes to selecting the right rental property, you must be mindful that the ones that you look at actually have good features that will make them profitable. Some people do not think far enough ahead when it comes time to invest, and as a result, they end up wasting money on an investment property that does not matter as much, and that can be a huge problem. When you want to invest in a rental property, you want it to actually turn a profit, and that can take time and effort.

When you are going to invest in a profitable rental property, you will need to consider certain features that will help you. You must make sure that any property that you choose is actually desirable enough to allow for that profit to be turned in the first place. There are several key factors that can help you to determine this.

Demand

First, you always want to ensure that your property is somewhere that there is actual demand. Supply and demand is something that is essential to you—if you want to make that money, you will need to purchase your rental somewhere that supply is low to allow for demand to go up. When there is a high demand for real estate somewhere, you will find that there are telltale signs, such as having low vacancy rates. When vacancy rates are low, and demand is high, you will be able to charge more money for the unit or house that you intend to rent out. This will allow you to lower the rate of vacancy as well. This is one of the best ways that you will be able to ensure that your property will allow you to make those return investments.

Jobs in the area

When you are looking at purchasing a house to rent out, one of the biggest drivers of demand will be the job market in the area that you choose to invest in. You might want to consider, for example, whether the job market is stable or what kinds of jobs are available to the tenants that will be there. For example, if you are near a hospital, you know that you can rent out properties to nurses or doctors who might be traveling through the area or who may only be working a short period in that particular area. This is important—knowing what kinds of jobs there available can help you figure out what the best investments will be. If you are looking to purchase property in areas where there are many agricultural workers, for example, you may see that rentals go for less money than they would if they were in a city full of technological hubs, such as Seattle or San Francisco.

The purchase price versus rental income

You need to consider the amount that you can charge for your rental property so you can figure out if the purchase price can be supported. If you choose to purchase somewhere where the going market for rent is $1500 for a two-bedroom house, but your mortgage on the house is $1900 per month, you are underwater on your investment. You can lose money if you are not careful about the rental income and how much you are looking to profit. You must make sure that you choose out properties that will work well for you and ensure that you will get the right amount of money to make it worthwhile. You must make sure that you've got the right price difference. If you play your cards right, you can find that you are highly successful. But, one misstep can destroy your chances of successful investment.

Features of a Profitable Commercial Property

Of course, you also have to be mindful of what kind of rental property you would develop as well. If you want to invest in commercial real estate, you need to know what you are doing, and you need to pick out the right kind of property. If you can do this, you will find that it is highly successful. If you want to ensure that you have a profitable commercial property, you must take the time to choose the investments carefully. You will need to ensure that the choices that you make are good. When it comes to choosing out commercial properties, you will need to follow certain standards as well. Of course, the commercial properties have far more regulations that you will have to mind as well. You must make sure that you choose out the investments that you make carefully.

Choosing out the location

One of the first considerations of your commercial property is the location. Where is it that you wish to invest? You want to make sure that you invest in a location where there is actual demand. You should have a demand for your commercial property. This means that if you were to buy a commercial property that is in the middle of nowhere, you would probably find that there is not much that you can do. You might find that you do not really profit much in that instance and that can be a major problem for you. That property may not see much in terms of traffic if it is difficult to get to. Most people don't want to drive too far out to get to locations like restaurants or stores. This means that unless someone offers something that is highly compelling, most businesses will struggle.

Location matters—you need to choose somewhere that is going to be beneficial. Choose somewhere that is easily accessed and somewhere that you are likely to find people who want to rent. You want to make sure that the property that you choose is going to actually be desired by someone who wants to run their business there. The best locations are those that are easily accessible to roads or freeways. They are commonly near other amenities as well, such as in a shopping district or in a mall.

Zoning considerations

Of course, it is not as simple as just buying a property and deciding to use it commercially. Otherwise, you would see people opening up convenience stores, restaurants, and the like in neighborhoods that are meant for living in. Property and real estate are typically zoned for specific uses. You can find properties that are specifically meant to be used for residential purposes, but also properties that are specifically zoned to allow for commercial uses.

Though it should go without saying, making sure that the properties that you choose out are also zoned accordingly is essential. If you purchase a property and only realize after the fact that it is not zoned in a way that you intended to use, you may struggle to sell it off, and you will not be able to use it for your intended purpose.

Physical condition of the property

The property that you choose to invest in needs to be in good condition. You must make sure that you choose your property that is either something that is already in good condition or is something that will need to be repaired, but the repairs are not so detrimental that they make the property worthless. When you keep in mind the physical condition, you want to ensure that the structure itself is sound. This means guaranteeing that everything is working and making sure that everything works well. Make sure that your property passes inspection and is in desirable condition before purchasing, or have a plan to get it in good condition before purchasing.

A common consideration that people may not make is liability issues that properties might have. For example, does your property prospect have asbestos or lead? Is the sidewalk or parking lot outside of the building risky? Are the pipes working? Are there stairs, escalators, or elevators that may need servicing? These are all considerations that you will need to make.

Parking availability

Another common consideration that many people don't think about when it comes to the desirability of a commercial property is the availability of parking. When you purchase a property to invest in, parking is a must. This is because the renters of your commercial property will naturally want somewhere that allows for their customers or clients to park. Is there street parking? A parking lot? These are important considerations to make. If you are purchasing a large building, is there parking to back it up? Having ample parking makes your property that much more desirable for those looking to rent out a location.

Flexibility

Finally, consider the flexibility of the property. You want to think about what it is that the property that you are in could need. You want to make sure that, for example, a property either has room to expand or room to be separated out. What if, for example, you realized that the property is too big for one little store? Could you cut it down? Could you put up a wall to separate it into two smaller properties relatively easily? Or, perhaps you want to make sure that your building is something that you could use for a restaurant, but also for a retail space later on. When you have a flexible property, you will be able to enjoy far more tenancy. When your property is flexible, you have the benefit of being able to use it for just about anything.

Chapter 7: Tips and Tricks to Selling Properties with Ease

Of course, so far, we have been talking more about what you can do to maintain your property rather than what you would do if you sold it off. However, for many people, there becomes an inevitable point at which you are ready to sell. You may have seen your property grow in value, but now, it is time to go over what you will need to do when it is time to sell your property. When it is time to sell, there are certain considerations that you can make to help you turn it around quickly. Are you looking to flip a property that you have invested in? Are you trying to cash in on your investment now that your property has matured over time? If so, you are in the right place—and the time is right to sell. All you will have to do is make sure that you are on the right track.

Now, of course, you could involve a real estate agency and have them take care of everything, so you do not have to be bothered with it, or you could also take the time to do it yourself. Generally speaking, if you want the biggest return, you get that by making sure that you are putting in the most effort. Usually, the more work that you put in yourself, the more money that you save on costs associated with outsourcing the work. This means that if you were to go through these steps on your own, you should find that you will actually see improvements in your properties selling, especially if you did your due diligence and made sure that you chose out properties that would be desirable. If you did that well, you would find that selling off the properties becomes easier than ever by putting these different tips to work as well.

Consider this chapter your guide to ensuring that you have everything that you will need to sell quickly. Whether you are selling quickly because you are ready to move, or if you are simply cashing in on your own investments, the rules of selling a house remain the same. Houses do not become inherently more marketable because it was your second property that you held onto for work or because you are taking the time to sell off your family home that you no longer need. You will still want to go through the same simple steps to ensure that you are on the right track and to maximize your investment.

Cleaning and Decluttering

The first step of selling any property is the cleaning and decluttering stage. At this stage, you will be taking a look at what you can do to clean up the property. After all, no one wants to buy a home that looks like it has seen better days or like it has not been taken care of unless they are planning on flipping it. If you want your property to be marketable enough to sell quickly, you want to ensure that you keep it spick and span.

If you are selling a property that is currently used as a rental property and there are tenants within it under the lease, you might want to consider talking to them and asking them about cleaning up their living space for you. If it is a property that you currently live in, you want to make sure that it is as clutter-free as possible. This means making sure that you put away anything that might cause crowding or messiness in the home. There are a few key tips and tricks that people use to prepare their properties for selling with ease, including:

- Putting all unnecessary items into storage. This allows you to make the rooms less crowded and make it appear to be more spacious.
- Organize closets and pantries. Because buyers that intend to live in a property will always look at the space available, you want the closets and pantries to look clean and provide the individual with a view of everything that they will be looking for. This will help them to envision what it is that they can do with space and will give a clearer idea of what space could be like for them. Plus, making sure that it is not cluttered in the storage spaces will help you to give the impression of having ample space.
- Put away all personal belongings. Things such as family photos or religious items tend to be distracting to buyers,

especially if they do not identify with the religion. This is because they make it harder for the individual to see themselves in that home.
- Deep clean, every single room. This means making sure baseboards, cabinets, tiles, and carpets are clean. If you find that you are running short on time, you might want to also consider calling for professionals to take care of it. You want the best foot forward with your property to ensure that the people want to live in it.

Invest in Minor Repairs

Along with making sure that the property is approachable and desirable in appearance, you may want to consider making basic repairs. This doesn't mean that you have to go in and do all of the bigger fixes, but you can still make sure that smaller repairs are taken care of. Many of these tasks can be completed quickly without much effort—you may, for example, take the time to patch up paint or fix loose tiles and squeaky or leaky faucets. By taking the time to do this, you make the house look that much nicer—it makes the people think that the property that they are getting is that much more desirable. Plus, those small repairs can start to build up and could even make or break a deal, depending upon what the competition is. When it comes to repairing and minor upgrades, consider the following:

- Apply a fresh coat of paint for the interior. This brightens up the room and makes it look cleaner.
- Install new hardware on cabinets. This will help to make the area look nicer and newer.
- Switch out outdated light fixtures. These are not very expensive but can do wonders to the way that the house looks.
- Match appliances. This is not something that everyone will do, but having new, matching appliances is a great way to boost appeal.

Staging and Boosting Curb Appeal

With just a single weekend of work, you can stage and boost curb appeal to help your house sell quicker and for a better price. You want to make a good impression on those coming to view your house, and because of that, you will need to pay close attention to how you present the house. According to the Zillow Group Report, 48% of buyers state that having a home already prepared and staged is very important to their decision when they purchase. It helps to figure out what to expect in the house and gives some context to space as opposed to just seeing it empty. When you have furniture and the like staged, you can get a better feel for what space really is and how it would be to live there. Between staging and landscaping outdoors, you can actually help your house sell better.

When you stage, you work to make rooms look larger. This is done the most effectively by paying a professional stager to come in and stage and decorate the home in a way that is appealing. They will work to make sure that the house looks as appealing as possible to get people to purchase it.

Because the first thing that people see of your house is the exterior, the best thing that you can do is show people the best that you can. Make sure that potential buyers get the best view in the beginning so that they can ensure that they are getting a good property. You need to have an exterior that looks maintained and clean while still being welcoming. Some of the best improvements for curb appeal that you can make include:

- Trimming hedges, branches, and shrubs
- Clearing paths and walkways
- Shining and cleaning windows and doorknobs
- Sweeping the porch and making sure it is free of spider webs or leaf litter
- Replace any broken or burnt out lights
- Paint the door
- Plant some flowers

Picking Your Strategy and Sticking to It

When you are ready to sell your property, you have several different options, but it really helps you to streamline the process if you figure out a strategy and stick to it. By making sure that you know how you are going to sell and making sure that you stick to that strategy, you can ensure that you are on the right track. You can, for example, choose to sell on your own or with an agent, or you can also figure out other options as well. The primary options that you have are:

- **For sale by owner:** This can be a lot of work, but you can save money. Commission for realtors is usually 3% of the price of the house, which can get awfully expensive if you are looking at houses with higher values. In Seattle, for example, the median price of a single-family home is $760,000. When you take 3% of that for the buyer's agent and 3% for your agent, you get a total of $22,800 per realtor, for a total of $45,600, which is nearly the median household income in the United States—just to sell a house. When you sell your house yourself, you can cut out that 3% for your agent, allowing you to pocket those savings. However, you need to be prepared to negotiate timelines, take care of contracts, and make sure that you get an attorney to look through the paperwork to make sure that everything is sound.
- **Hiring an agent:** Conventionally, people prefer to hire an agent to take care of their sale for them. The agent is able to take care of all paperwork, prep work, negotiations, and closing. However, that comes at a cost—the 3% mentioned previously.
- **Sell to investors:** You could also sell your home to an investor for a quick offer, usually in cash form, rather than having to wait for a mortgage company to approve everything.
- **Sell to developers:** If your property is in a state of disrepair, you can also choose to sell it to a developer who may decide to tear the whole things down and develop it themselves.

- **Auction your home:** Usually, people can auction off homes rapidly to get their house off the market quicker—but you usually do so at a price. Auctioned houses are regularly less than what you would get if you had listed it traditionally.

Knowing the Price and Pricing Accordingly

A problem that many sellers run into is that they feel like they cannot get their property off the market quickly enough. Even when selling in a seller's market, you can run into issues if your house is simply not competitive enough. Some houses, especially when they are not well maintained or they are not priced properly, may linger on the market. The best realtor in the world is not going to be able to sell a house that is priced far too high for the location and what it is. You need to make sure that you know how much your property is worth and what you can do about it. When you are able to plan accordingly and price things out fairly, you will probably sell quicker.

Now, you might think that you could just price it at a higher cost and take lower—but if you do this, you may miss several on the market, and you will end up selling lower anyway. Why not just price it for what you want and expect it to sell? In fact, many realtors currently recommend that you price your home a little but underneath comparable homes because doing so will get interested in your house, and interest can lead to a bidding war if two people find your home and decide that it will be perfect for you. Of course, this is highly dependent upon the market that you are attempting to sell in.

When you set your price, you must also consider the price points that people are looking for. If $400,000 is a median price in your area, you might not bat an eye at pricing your home at $405,000. But, you need to consider that this will also likely cut out several people. Many people may never see your property if they are looking for homes at and under $400,000. You might want to consider pricing at $399,000 instead. By pricing with $9,000 at the end of your price, you will be able to undercut many different boundaries and in the grand scheme of things, when you are talking about hundreds of thousands of dollars, $1,000 gone to sell quicker is not usually a deal-breaker for people.

Additionally, you need to consider your timeline that you want to sell within. When do you want to drop your price? Figure out what that first timeline will be at which you would drop the price if you do not get any offers. You can choose the amount that you will drop the price later, but if you find that your house is not selling, you will probably want to lower the cost. This is because the longer a home lingers, the less likely it is to sell at the cost offered for it.

If you are not sure how quickly your property will sell, you can also sell with incentives that are meant to make people feel better about buying your property. This could be something such as offering credits for improvements or upgrading something at the buyer's request. When you sweeten the deal, you make your home more desirable. One of the most common is including appliances with the home, especially because doing so is not a guarantee when selling houses. Some people just want to take their appliances with them to a new house.

Professional Photography

Though it is cheaper and easier to simply take pictures of your house yourself, the truth is that photos that are not professional grade will lead to your home sitting for far longer than you intended. According to the Zillow Group Report, 77% of buyers say that professional photography is important to their home-buying decision. These services are not always incredibly pricy, but they can leave a lasting impact on the property that you are trying to sell. If you can, use the few hundred dollars to pay for professional photography, and if possible, include a 3D virtual house tour—these work great to boost sales for the house, especially in the current climate with the 2020 pandemic. By providing a professional virtual tour, people can walk through the house from the comfort of their own homes, which can help boost interest or morale for a house.

When your photos are taken with the help of a photographer, you get the added bonus of being able to get the best lighting and staging in your photos. Make sure that you schedule this appointment at a good time to allow natural light to flow through your house to create a lighter, brighter appearance.

Create a Listing Description

When you have your listing price and all of your staging and photography taken care of, it is time to get that good listing description set up. You want your description to be perfect to showcase what you really value about your house. Make sure that you talk about what you love and highlight the best features. Make use of good keywords and do anything that you can to create a compelling description of the home.

Of course, this means that all amenities or local benefits, such as being near a park, being near schools, or public transportation, all matter. Make sure that you discuss why you love your home and why you believe that the new buyer would want to live there. Of course, this is mostly dependent upon your desired audience that you have in mind.

Within your description, make sure that you also include urgency within it—make sure that the people feel like they don't want to miss out. When you put a deadline for offers to be submitted, you create that sense of urgency that will help light that fire that will motivate the buyers to act quickly—when something has a concrete deadline at which the offer no longer stands, they are more likely to feel compelled to simply jump at the option.

Timing the Sale Just Right

It has been shown that the best time to post your house for sale is the first half of May on a Saturday. When you do this, you will see that homes sell on average, six days quicker, and for $1,600 more than they otherwise would. This is important to keep in mind—when you have the flexibility to list when it is the most beneficial for you, this will do it, but that also means that you might have to hold until that point in time.

You might be wondering what it is about that time that makes selling houses so compelling, and the answer is simple—when you sell at that time, you are actually catching on with the people looking to move over the summer. Think about it—moving over the summer means less disruption to the school year, especially for people who may be moving from further away. This timeline makes perfect sense when you consider that winters are usually packed with busyness, from being worried about schools, the holidays, and even inclement weather. In many areas within the United States, there are times of the year that would simply be too dangerous to move during. This means that if you want to ensure that you can sell your house quicker, you will need to consider the time of year that you will sell.

Be Flexible with Showings

Finally, the last tip that will help you to sell your property quickly is to be flexible with the showings. When you sell quickly, you need to be accommodating. Doing so will help you to ensure that people are more likely to come view. Yes, it can be a struggle to deal with last-minute or short-notice showings, but people are not going to buy if they cannot walk in! If you are not going to accommodate the schedules of the buyers, you are not likely to sell quickly. Along with that general flexibility, however, you have some other considerations to make.

For example, you might want to hold an open house. Especially if you time it well on the weekend, you can get several people through the door. Because there is no need to schedule, you may be pleasantly surprised that you get far more traffic than you expected. However, you will want to make sure that you keep in mind that this is not the only way to show your house.

You will also want to ensure that you have private showing availability as well. Now, most realtors will not try to get you to show at strange times that might be difficult to accommodate, such as late at night or exorbitantly early in the morning. However, the reality is that if you are attempting to sell your property, you want to do so effectively, and you will want to make sure that you have that availability to ensure that people can see your home. Keep in mind that if you are selling yourself without a realtor, you will have to host the tours. However, if you work with an agent, they will host for you or allow for a lockbox for the buyer and their agent to walk through. Keep in mind that if you are going to be showing, you should not be present, if at all possible. Typically, having the owner present makes the showing more uncomfortable and can hurt your chance at selling.

Finally, you want to consider pocket listing. This occurs when you have a well-connected agent spreading the word about your home coming on the market to other agents before listing. This allows you to begin to build up interest and potentially even sell a home before it has ever been officially listed. If your house is desirable enough and you get lucky enough, you can even get an offer before having to list at all, saving lots of time, energy, and money.

Chapter 8: Real Estate Crowdfunding

Another common form of investing that has been growing in popularity recently is real estate crowdfunding. Maybe you are interested in gaining the benefits from real estate, recognizing that they can make a massive amount of cash, but you are also not really interested in spending all of that time working on the harder parts. If this sounds like you, you are not alone, but thankfully, you have another option for you. You can use real estate crowdfunding to help boost your portfolio without having to worry so much about other people.

Crowdfunding works a bit differently than many other options. Instead of buying property, you are funding businesses. It is an easier way to get involved in real estate. The idea behind this form of investment is simple—it is that you will not have to invest so much to get a good return. Think about it—it is hard to find people that will invest a higher amount of money. Not many people have enough money sitting around to simply purchase a whole property without a mortgage. However, many people can put down a smaller amount of money. Crowdfunding plays off the idea that several people can invest smaller amounts of money and that those smaller amounts of money can build up enough to allow for a purchase of a property.

Crowdfunding can be somewhat off-putting to certain people, but it has its own time and place that you ought to consider. When you make use of crowdfunding, you invest slightly differently than any of the other ways that we have discussed thus far. There are some distinct differences that can make this form of investment highly promising, but there are some reasons that you may hesitate when it comes to choosing these options for yourself. Within this chapter, you can expect to gain information about what crowdfunding is and how it works, as well as the benefits and limitations that you can run into. You will also see some important details, such as investment limits and what the primary differences are between REITs and crowdfunding, both of which may sound quite similar at first glance. Is this form right for you? Maybe—but you will have to decide that for yourself.

What is Real Estate Crowdfunding and How Does it Work?

Crowdfunding is a way of raising money for properties—typically businesses—to gain property. It also allows for people to invest and make a profit as well. The idea here is that there are some people who may not be able to afford a commercial property that they need to open their own business. In lacking that property, they are going to struggle to ever open up their business. However, with crowdfunding, they are able to make up that money.

Typically. Crowdfunding works by reaching out across the internet to reach several potential investors. Those investors may be willing to invest smaller amounts of money, which, on their own, may not be enough to purchase a property, but if they were to get several investors with those smaller amounts of funding, they would be able to invest properly. This is the goal here—to get those investors ready and willing to spend the cash. This is a win-win for both sides—the investors get to become shareholders in a company or property for significantly less than they normally would have to spend, and the companies are able to gain access to the funding that they needed to get off the ground.

Crowdfunding works thanks to the fact that small- and mid-sized companies can gain the money they need that will boost the companies' chances of surviving. Traditionally, this happened with equity transactions—in which accredited investors were able to spend the money needed to buy shares of the company. Accredited investors are any series of banks, pension plans, insurance companies, and wealthy investors. Typically, for an individual to be considered an investor, they must have a net worth of over $1,000,000.

Equity investments have changed somewhat in recent days, however—now, there are options for people to be able to purchase and own a smaller share of the company or property. Investors can get just a portion of the profits just by putting in the money, and they do to have to put up a massive amount of money. In some cases, it is the case that people can become shareholders for just $5,000. This is good news for beginner investors that do not have hundreds of thousands of dollars.

Benefits of Crowdfunding

Of course, crowdfunding gets as much attention as it does because it is highly beneficial. Many people recognize that the truth is that this is a fantastic way to begin investing in real estate without having the ability to buy a property. It is a great way to gain a foothold in real estate, and over time, you can work to start investing your own funds that you get in return toward purchasing more real estate. It is a great method that you can use to start benefitting if you only have a few thousand dollars free.

In some cases, there is a small minimum to invest in the company—usually between $1000 and $5000. That amount is meant to keep this form of investment accessible to most people interested in investing in the first place. This is great news for you if that is your hope.

It is also the case that if the company does go public, meaning that they start selling stock to the public via the stock market or something similar, you can start making massive investment gains. This is because you get a share of the profits thanks to your status as a crowdfunding investor. If the company that you have invested in is suddenly sharing massive amounts of money, you can benefit from that.

One of the greatest benefits of this form of investment, however, is the fact that when you choose to invest in crowdfunding, you do not have to worry about the traditional real estate investment problems. You are not on the hook for traditional investment costs, such as closing costs or realtor commissions—you are simply giving a portion of the money to a company and then being able to get that return over time. This is easy money for most people and allows for a significant amount of profit.

Disadvantages of Crowdfunding

Of course, where there is potential to earn money, there is potential for risk as well. The most profitable ventures usually are the ones that will be the highest risk, and that is a huge problem for many people. If you are risk-averse, this is probably not the method of investment for you just due to the fact that you are putting money into a company that is fairly new or unknown. If the company is requiring crowdfunding to make ends meet to get that property, there is a good chance that the company either has a rocky financial history or it does not have much of one at all. This means that if the company goes under, you could lose everything and not have any recourse to get it back. If you do not know what you are doing, you can end up losing a massive amount of money, and if you invest in these companies and the companies fail, then you could simply lose everything in one go.

Of course, there is also the downside that for some projects, you will have to be accredited, or at the very least, incredibly wealthy, to make these investments work for you. Think about it—if you have a limit of just $2,200 per year that you can invest, you cannot get very far as someone that is not accredited. Of course, you would be able to invest more in other ways as well, but that limitation means that you cannot count on this form of investment for your primary mode of making money if you do not have a massive amount of income right off the bat.

Investment Limits

Of course, with all of those benefits and with how this form of investment works, there has to be some sort of regulation that will help to ensure that the property is funded successfully. Thanks to the risks involved in this form of investment, there are several limits that have been implemented by the Securities and Exchange Commission (SEC) on non-accredited investors. Most beginners will not be accredited, and that means that they may be a very serious risk. There are limits based on the income that will control just how much of your money that you will invest at any point in time.

This might sound patronizing or paternalistic, but it is in the interest of the investors. By limiting the amount of money that can be invested at any given point in time, the people have that protection to keep from losing a massive amount of money. The limits are based on the number of $107,000.

If your annual income is underneath this number, or if your net worth is underneath this number, then you have a very specific limit to your investments. During any 12-month period, you can invest either $2,200 or 5% of your annual income or net worth—whichever is lower. This means that if you make $107,000 per year, you can only invest $2,200. If you make $29,000 per year, you can invest just $1,450 per year. This is to protect you from losing money that you cannot afford to lose.

Over $107,000 helps raise the limits a bit—at this income bracket, you can invest up to 10% of your annual income or net worth. This can never exceed $107,000, so if you want to invest more than that, you will need to get accreditation. Of course, most people will not have that problem when it comes to their own investments—very few people will ever seriously be hit by that income cap.

REITs vs. Crowdfunding

At the end of the day, there is actually a difference between REITs and crowdfunding. They both operate in very similar manners in the sense that you will have money being invested in a property without having to purchase the whole thing, but they also vary significantly as well. In particular, REITs will work by allowing you to invest in commercial property while then receiving returns through the form of dividends. Crowdfunding, however, skips this.

Crowdfunding allows entrepreneurs to build up the money they need for projects from several people. This allows you to begin investing in real estate without having to actually be involved in the property. And, any profits from the venture, such as through rental income or through flipping the property get returned to you, the investor.

Though similar, they do have those key differences. While REITs provide dividends, creating a guaranteed income, and are easy to trade, crowdfunding does not share that benefit. You receive a portion of the profits rather than a set dividend, meaning that the return that you get will be highly dependent upon the kind of success that the property that you invested in returns. With those differences in mind, then, you might think that REITs are a better option, and in some cases, they are lower risk and easier to sell. With crowdfunding, you are a shareholder on the property and you own a certain amount of the property itself. With REITs, you invest in a company that then turns around profits by investing in companies. Ultimately, what is best for you is the choice that you will have to make yourself. You will have to figure out what is going to work better for you so you can invest intelligently. However, the hope is that whatever it is, you will benefit well.

Is Crowdfunding Worth it?

The bottom line is that while real estate can be a wonderful form of investment, it can also be quite difficult to manage. If you want to crowdfund, you have the potential to make a massive amount of money. However, you will also have to work hard to ensure that you are on track. You will need to make sure that you are capable of providing the right amount of funding to ensure that you can actually make a reasonable amount of profit. If you cannot provide that amount of funding, then this is little more than just another method that you can use to diversify your own portfolio.

Now, remember—diversification of your portfolio is essential to success. If you want to make sure that you can diversify, then this is a wonderful option. However, depending upon what you are doing, you might find that this simply is not worth it for you. This can be a great way to make money, but it is also highly regulated and you will have to follow guidelines to ensure that your investment is allowed the way that it is. If you want to follow through with these forms of investment, you can do so—but you want to proceed with caution rather than going full steam ahead.

Chapter 9: Common Failures Beginners Face

Real estate is risky. It is, in many cases, incredibly risky. It is estimated that upwards of 90% of real estate investors fail. This means that out of every ten investors, only one is going to actually make it. For the other 9? They may simply throw in the towel and give up before it gets too bad. Others may find themselves so overleveraged that they have no idea what they can do to protect themselves. Others still may find themselves bankrupted or in complete and utter financial ruin. Real estate has an incredible amount of risk, and that, when paired with the low barrier of entry to get into the field, leads to a massive amount of failures. The astronomical failure rate can be unnerving—and it should be. This should give you pause and make you think about what you are doing. You should wonder if this is right for you.

If you are having second thoughts right now, then great! That's perfect! This is not a business to get into lightly. It is imperative that you sit down and thoroughly weigh your options here before getting involved. If you fail to do so, you show a lack of foresight that could potentially spell trouble for you later on. The best investors know when to consider risk, and they know when to back away.

Unfortunately, despite the fact that there is no perfectly risk-free investment, real estate remains among some of the riskiest, even if you take the time to go through and work hard to minimize it. You stand a very real chance of struggling with your investment—it is entirely possible, and even statistically probable, that you will fail. Are you still interested?

If so, then great—you have to have the right mindset, and that mindset must be determined to make everything work for you. Of course, you are probably curious about what it is that will up your failure rate. And the truth is—it's not nice. There are five common mistakes that people tend to ignore that can spell significant trouble for investors like you looking to get started. Sure, all you really need to do is go out there and put down the money. It is easy to read a book and then decide "I'm a flipper now," especially if you have the funding to back your desires. But, if you don't have the right mindset, you will fail.

If you are looking to make the best choices for yourself to ensure that you can succeed in your own real estate market, then you are in the right place. This chapter is here to provide you with several of the most common failures and mistakes that beginners make when it comes to real estate. There are, unfortunately, several that you will need to consider to ensure that you are more successful. These mistakes are highly serious to manage well and prevent so you can up your chances. After all, the odds are currently stacked up against you—you will have to do something that will protect you and turn things back in your own favor—even if just a little bit.

Following Emotions Instead of Numbers

Before you do anything with an investment, you owe it to yourself to stop and calculate out the return on investment for that particular investment. Are you going to profit? If you think with your feelings instead of with your brain, you can run into some serious risks. Investors who tend to fail in real estate are those who will invest based on their feelings. They might see a property and fall in love with it. They can see it as beautiful or wonderful in some way, and because of that, they open their wallets and put down the money—but they do so without thinking about the repercussions. They do so without thinking about what they could do to protect their investment. Is the investment unintelligent? It might be—if they are looking to invest money based on a whim rather than whether they can actually make money on it, they are going to fail.

Now, you might say, "but the property is perfect!" and it might be—for you. But, if it is not a good investment for other reasons, such as being in a poor location, or because your tastes are very niche and you are going to have a hard time finding someone who thinks or sees similarly to you, you are going to struggle. Consider the fact that if you want to put in an investment, you need to look at it logically. No one else cares that the property that you are looking at, in that ugly shade of chartreuse with the lime green carpet, is the coolest house ever and that you have the perfect idea of what you would do with it and how you could spin it to be fantastic. People are going to see it and think that it is *awful*. And, the lack of offers or renters will speak for itself.

You cannot allow your emotions to influence your business venture. It is time to think with your mind, not your heart, and that means making sure that no matter what you do, you ensure that you are buying properties or investing in ones that you can be certain are going to return on their investments. This means that you will have to work harder to ensure that you can and will make money.

Failing to Dedicate Time

Next, consider how much time it will take for you to make money. Now, there are several options that may be quicker than others, but none of them will make you rich overnight, and none of them are going to be entirely effortless. You put in effort one way or another, whether that is through working to pay for the bill for a management company or in sweat equity while you work to provide everything that your investment will need. This is perhaps one of the most common failures that people run into.

People fail when they do not put in enough time to their project. Remember this—you are investing. You are actively putting something into your project with the hopes that, in the end, you will turn a profit. This is, by definition, the effort that you have to exert. It's simplistic to feel like all you have to do is set and forget your money and wait for it to grow. If that was what you wanted, there are options that allow for that—and they are not stocks. Usually, if you want to do that, you will be taking a look at methods such as investing in ETFs or even REITs. But, for the most part, real estate will not afford you such luxury to allow you to simply put down the money and walk away.

Of course, putting in time doesn't mean just being there to act either—it means putting time in to focus on what matters. You need to focus if you want to succeed, and most people seem to miss this point. They don't realize that what they really need to do is sit back and schedule in time for what matters to them, and if what matters the most to them is their goals, then they need to make them a priority.

What most people think of as putting in the time is highly insufficient—they may say, "Well, I read that book online!" or "I spent 30 minutes looking for new properties." However, these are not proper investment options—you need to make sure that you are putting in the time and effort to properly do so in other ways. Putting in the time and effort that you will need to succeed involves doing more. It means that you are serious about what you are doing and will allow you to start making a decent return just by knowing what to do next.

If you are not willing to work yourself to the ground for the next year or year and a half, then you may be in the wrong field. This is not simple or easy. It is not something that you can simply stumble upon and tell yourself that you will succeed. It is something that will take hard work—and sometimes even require you to forego gratification at the moment to ensure that you create something larger. Do not waste time to give up, and at the same time, you should never give up on a dream just because you think it will take too long to actually succeed.

The best investments require you to work hard. They require you to take the time to really push yourself forward and make sure that ultimately, you are taking the time and effort to succeed. If you want to do so, then you can—and it all starts with making sure that you work hard.

Quitting Prematurely

Now, if it is important to know that you should quit if you are not fully invested, it might seem strange that the next failure would be one of quitting too soon. But, the truth is that without perseverance and without being able to properly put blood, sweat, and tears into what you are doing, you will struggle. You need to be willing and able to stick to it and persevere when times get tough. Times *will* get tough somewhere along the way—real estate is not, by any means, simple or easy to get into. But, what it is is something that you can use to better yourself. You can use it to ensure that at the end of the day, you are working for something bigger and better than yourself. When you do this appropriately and accordingly, you will find that you can succeed.

Of course, this is something that is, to some degree, simply brain chemistry. Did you know that some people, particularly those with higher levels of dopamine, may have a higher drive to persevere while those with lower dopamine levels, are more inclined to give up? Now, that doesn't mean that you have an excuse to simply throw in the towel and say that you are done—it means that you need to accept that you might have to work harder to make this work for you. It could be the case that you have to try harder, and you will have to work with yourself to figure out how best to keep yourself on track.

Giving up is almost immediately akin to failure—all because you cannot possibly succeed if you have quit. This means that one of the biggest failures that beginners face is simply throwing in the towel because things got tough. But, remember—the best things are not easy by any means. Sometimes, you have to suffer. Sometimes, you have to work harder to ensure that you can succeed. Sometimes, you have to ensure that you work just a bit more to ensure that you can get past the difficulty and move on. If you want to succeed, you can do so—you just have to have the perseverance in the first place.

Not Focusing

Another common issue is a lack of focus. You might say, "I'm focusing on too many different properties." But what does that imply? You cannot focus on too many. That is contradictory. To focus is to have a specific center of activity or a point at which you are paying attention. You cannot focus on too many things at the same time—that is the very definition of unfocused! Of course, in real estate investment, there are many different ways you can go. Do you want to flip properties while also renting out some and investing in REITs while trying to run an Airbnb? If so, hopefully you have a lot of time on your hands and do not have to worry about other things as well because that plate is already overflowing!

It is difficult to focus when it comes to real estate—but you have to find that point of focus. You have to figure out where it is that you can focus more so you can succeed. If you can do this, you should find yourself thriving. Real estate investors who do not focus on just one or two projects often find themselves failing. You cannot succeed if you are not focused and clear about what you are doing or how you are going to do it.

Ironically, if you had some early successes in your investment career, you probably find yourself struggling to focus more. You may have several people who want different things from you—but you fail to do any of them well because none of them are your core point of expertise. This means that you are going to struggle more—you are going to find yourself failing to actually make things work for you just because you have to let your mind go several different directions instead of just one.

When you have your mind going a million different ways, you will struggle to focus more. You will struggle to think of what it is that you really need to do and if you do struggle that way, you will find yourself setting up for failure. As an investor, you will have to do something right to ensure that you are safe. You will have to focus and say no to opportunities if those opportunities are not exactly what you were looking to do. It is okay to turn down projects or tasks if they are not going to help you directly better yourself or your future. It is okay for you to reject the idea of working in fields or investments that are not going to benefit you. What is not okay, however, is to allow yourself to drown because you are too afraid to say no.

Skipping Education

Now, you might think that since investing in real estate does not have any minimum window beyond simply having the money that you need, that you can get by without needing any sort of formal training. Now, while you don't need to spend a fortune on real estate material, you still cannot go into the process entirely uneducated. So many people fail because they never learn what they need to know to thrive. They never learn what they will need to do to successfully navigate the world around them and that can be a major problem for just about anyone. If you want to succeed, you need to make sure that you take the time to get educated.

Skip those seminars that promise to make you rich quickly—they will not help you here. What you need is a real, genuine education on the subject. Take the time to educate yourself, and if you are reading this right now, you are already on the right foot! Keep it up! The more that you do, the better you will do! You don't have to spend a ton of money to learn what you will need—you just have to take the time to read.

You can also get to know more about the business in other simple manners. You could, for example, choose to meet up with other realtors. You could go on forums and talk to people. You could join groups to meet up with other professionals and pick their brains for a while. Being able to get access to other people and their expertise is a wonderful way to ensure that you know what you are doing and that what you are doing is going to be successful for you.

Skipping the Business Aspect and Skills

Finally, the last major failure for people is that of failing to learn the business aspect of everything. Keep in mind that you are not simply an investor here—you need to understand how to run your business as well. Are you going to work hard to ensure that you understand the business side of things?

Think about it—if you are investing in flipping properties, do you understand the more technical information that you will need to know? Do you understand what you will have to do related to the flipping of the process? Yes, you will need those real estate skills. You will need to understand the paperwork, the terms, the investments, and how to turn that profit. But, there is more to it as well. You must understand what you are doing so you can be certain that you are also turning a profit.

Did you know that of small businesses, which you would be counted as if you were flipping houses for profit, 46% of the failures is due to managerial incompetence? 20% is due to unbalanced expertise. 18% fail due to a lack of experience with management, and another 9% fail due to inexperience of the employees. 3% fail due to business neglect, 2% fail from fraud, 1% fail due to disaster, and 2% fail due to external factors that have nothing to do with the business itself. What does that say to you?

That says that 98% of small business failures come from a lack of business awareness or skill.

Yes, 98% of people who fail could have avoided failure if they had the right business skills to help them stay afloat. Most people seem to act like they can be successful if they simply build a website, spend some time on social media, read a few blog posts about what they can do to succeed, and move on. But, it is *never* that simple. You need the skill to back it up.

The reality is, if you are attempting to make money in real estate, whether as an investor yourself, or through any other means, you need the technical skill to keep yourself afloat and successful. No, it is not easy to make money online—the only people who will tell you that it is easy to start turning a profit online are those who want to sell you something. If you want to really succeed, you will need to ensure that you work effectively. You will need to think of some sort of way, shape, or form that you can prove to yourself and to those around you that you have the technical skill.

You need to understand how to market. You need to understand how to run a website and how to ensure that other people see your business and want to get involved. You need to be able to understand how all of this works and how you can thrive in doing so. There is a reason that business is a major field in the universities—it is hard to muster. It takes years to learn how to operate a business successfully and without those skills, you will fail.

The Bottom Line

Failure happens. It is a part of life and in fields like real estate, it happens more often than not. It is difficult to learn how to navigate around, but you will need to learn if you wish to succeed. Keep in mind that failure is not actually as bad as you might think—failure is the act of learning. You learn more when you fail than when you succeed. When you fail, you see what you can do different next time. Of course, in real estate, those failures can become quite pricy. Those failures can start to cost thousands, or even tens of thousands of dollars if you don't know what you are doing and that can be highly intimidating and off-putting. But, the truth is, those failures can help you.

Failure will be a part of the process—but you will need to learn to persevere past them. What can you do to succeed beyond those failures? What can you do to ensure that you are going to thrive in your setting? Whatever you do, you will need to be smart about it.

As you read through this chapter, you saw several different failures that will kill your business. We went over five different ways that you cannot afford to fail and how you can get around them. The truth is, real estate will always be difficult. It will always be hard for you to figure out, but if you can learn to navigate it, you can thrive.

Conclusion

And that brings us to the end of this journey! At this point, it is time to wrap up this book and move on. Hopefully, as you read through this book, you learned a wide range of information about what it takes to invest in real estate and how you can be highly successful with it if you know what you are doing. Do you want to learn how to make money on the market? Are you ready to put to use all of that information that it will take for you to successfully navigate the world around you? If so, then keep it up—you will succeed.

From this point forward, it is important for you to recognize what it is that you will need to do next. You need to learn about how you can properly and successfully navigate through the world of real estate. That can really only happen through sheer experience. Until you have done it yourself, you can never truly appreciate or understand what it is going to take for you to succeed. But you can get started now!

At this point, we've covered a wide range of topics that were designed to be beneficial to you. We've covered several different topics that will help you to understand precisely what you will need and how you can ensure that you turn around the profits that you are looking for. From learning about what to do and what to avoid to introductions to several different investment options that you have out there, you should have a pretty good idea of what you are interested in.

Before you get out there and start investing, really consider if this is the path that you want to go down. It may be—and that's great! But, if it is not something that you are comfortable with, you may want to consider some other options as well. You may want to consider what you can do differently to help yourself. You want to consider the risk that you are willing to endure and recognize that, at some point, you will lose money. We all do at one point or another. There are no perfect or safe investments out there—there are just relatively-safe investments. This means that you should not be investing more than you can afford.

Do not over-leverage yourself. Do not put yourself in more debt than you can afford to invest. Do not invest money that you cannot afford to lose. If you do so, you run an even more serious risk if you are not careful. Now, before we part, let's go over a list of recommendations for anyone considering real estate investments. If you are ready to invest, then remember these points to protect yourself and those you care about or who rely on you financially.

1. **Don't let your discouragement bring you down:** You will feel discouraged at some point, especially if you fail the first time around. If you don't learn from that failure, you have truly failed. If you have learned something, then you've succeeded in your own way.
2. **Don't have unrealistic expectations:** Remember that too many people out there like to push this idea that you can get rich quick with little to no investment. This is not true! You can't get rich quickly—but you can start learning how to invest and get rich eventually.
3. **It takes money to earn money:** If you want to build up wealth, you will have to invest money first. Most investments require you to buy and hold while renting. Unless you live somewhere with a high rate of inflation, you will probably be investing a significant amount of money while you build that property value up.
4. **Expect the market to crumble sometimes:** Sometimes, it is simply not a good market. Make sure that you navigate through those turbulent times with good renters that have been thoroughly and carefully vetted and screened.
5. **Have patience:** Things will take time to grow. Let yourself remember to be patient, and you will see great benefits. It will take time, but you can make money.
6. **Evaluate and criticize everything:** While you can't overthink things, you should also make sure that you think carefully about all of the activities that you may be interested in. You want to ensure that you are only ever investing in the best deals, and that means that you need to learn what it will

take for you to weigh the pros and cons along the way. Make sure that you criticize each and every point that you make.

And if you remember these points, you can succeed! Remember that things will not always go your way, but you can persevere. If at all possible at this point, consider finding a mentor—someone that is already quite experienced in the field and is willing to show you the ropes. If you can do this and learn how to recognize and evaluate any deals that you enter into, you should be able to make great progress with ease.

As you prepare to head off on your own personal real estate journey, remember that you are in for the long haul. Don't be afraid to acknowledge that what you are doing is going to take time and effort. Recognize the gravity of what you are preparing to get yourself into, and good luck out there!

Thank you for taking the time to read through this book. There are so many different guides to a real estate out there that promise you the answers to get rich quickly. But, the truth is, there is no real get the rich quick scheme. There is no real way for you to suddenly see that wealth explode. It is only with time, effort, and money that you can make that return that you are looking for—but you know how to get started now! Are you ready? Are you thinking about what you want to do next? Then, great! Get out there! Prepare yourself and start trying! And, hopefully, even though you may stumble, you will soon find that you are running with ease.

Good luck out there—and if you found that this book was useful to you, please consider leaving a review with your experience on Amazon to let others know what you think! Your feedback is always greatly appreciated!

www.ingramcontent.com/pod-product-compliance
Lightning Source LLC
Chambersburg PA
CBHW070455220526
45466CB00004B/1842